Creating Real Estate Riches

Maximizing Real Estates Profits Through
Trustee Sales and Foreclosures

Hung Q. Do
Khoa Le

Authority
PRESS

Published by Authority Press, Inc.
7777 N Wickham Rd, # 12-247
Melbourne, FL 32940
Authority-Press.com

Manufactured in the United States of America.

ISBN: 978-1-62865-067-9

Contents

Foreword

In my years of real estate experience, I have read many books about flipping homes and I am very impressed with *Create Real Estate Riches*, written by Hung Q. Do. This book provides a road map for both novice and experienced investors to create wealth from trustee sales to foreclosure homes.

I met Hung when I spoke at the Peak Potentials Never Work Again Seminar. Hung came across as very professional in his investment business. As I talked with Hung, I found out that he had a big dream to help millions of people better understand the process of flipping homes. I have heard many horror stories from my students and acquaintances of the challenges with flipping real estate due to their lack of experience, lack of systematic approaches, and lack of personal perseverance. All are essential to success in any business.

Hung not only shows you the fundamentals but takes you deep into the processes, approaches, tricks, tips, and techniques of flipping homes. He shares with you the ins and outs on how to deal with the local government, the construction companies, and the funding challenges you'll face to successfully make the investment. Reading this book will take you from a less-than ideal financial situation to financial freedom. It contains the secrets of building personal strength and wealth.

I am very happy to write the foreword for Hung's book. I know you will learn lot from the stories and lessons provided by herein.

Congratulations on choosing this book; I wish you great successes in your journey.

Raymond Aaron
NY Times Best Selling Author
www.aaron.com

Introduction

This book is a detailed step-by-step on how to acquire a property either from trustee sales or foreclosure then fixing it up, listing it, and making a profit. We wrote this book because the system we have developed will help many people establish their financial freedom or stabilize their financial situation.

Even though the book presents to you a detailed procedure, it is important that you experience the process on your own. What we present here is our own experience and story, which may or may not fit your situation. This much we know, it can definitely help you reach your financial goals.

With many successful people, you often hear about their story and how many of them have lost everything before they reached the success they are at today. I do not have such a sad story but I do have a story to share with you.

REI Invest was established in 2010 with the focus of helping investors get the highest return possible from the market using their retirement fund or extra cash. We also focus on educating our clients, big or small, on how to maximize their income for larger investment fund. We invest in real estate by flipping. We have a system where it allows us to find the best real estate deals out there with trustee sales. One of the most often asked questions is "How can one judge the success of a company and know that the company experts have the proper experiences?" Our track record will demonstrate this for you.

In 2010, the company used the system and was able to acquire, fix, and sell 165 properties. In 2011, we repeated the process and sold 268 properties. In 2012, we acquired 320 properties. We had an 87% selling rate and a 13% holding for assets building. These numbers are high marks and an indication of a strong growing company. These numbers also give us the encouragement to write this book and share our know-how with you. First let me share with you a bit about myself, Hung Q. Do, and about my partner, Khoa Le.

At the age of 14, I left my homeland of Vietnam as a refugee of war after the fall of Saigon, South Vietnam and came to America. My grandparents were farmers, my uncles were in the armed forces, my aunts were business owners, my father was a policeman, and my mother was an office administrator for an American import/export company. I was always interested in the business at a young age. However, with our culture, I was told to study hard to become a doctor, lawyer, or an engineer because they make good income. When we landed in Mexico, Missouri, I studied hard, had a paper route, worked as a dish washer at the local restaurant, and worked on my homework late into the night. The first winter in a new country, I started my first business which I did not know at the time – snow shoveling. The idea came to me when I woke up one morning and could not walk out of my house. We started to shovel the snow using the regular shovel and saw other people were doing the same. After I finished my tasks, I walked to the neighbor's house and asked if I can help them shovel the snow since most of my neighbors were elderly couples. They were happy that I asked and said yes. After I finished, they gave me five dollars for my effort. I was surprised because my intention was to help out without anything in return. At that moment, the business started. I talked to my brothers and within a few days, I had a team working for me shoveling snow. I paid them 3 dollars and kept 2 dollars for myself for the house they worked on. We had a lot of fun doing the shoveling because, while working, we were having snowball fights with the other neighborhood children as well. Some of the children asked to join our workforce. The dream of owning my own business stayed with me since then. The lesson here is to earn the money by leveraging the effort of others.

To obey my parents and to stay within our culture, I had put aside my business dream and I studied to become a special engineer and graduated from California State University of Hayward with a Bachelor of Science degree and minor in math. After graduation I spent almost a year looking for a job but landed on nothing. The answer I got from all the job searching was "you have no experience." "How can I get experience when I do not have opportunity to work?" I asked myself. Most businesses left me no answers. One mom-and-pop software company agreed to give me a chance to establish the experience needed but I had to work for free in the beginning to prove whether or not I had the capability. I worked hard and generated revenue of $20,000 monthly for them for six months before I received a salary of $9.00 an hour in 1982. While working as a software engineer, the business dream came back to me and because of the work load, I had to push it aside and just work hard at making money for the owner. One day, the hard reality came when I overheard the owner say "Everyone is expendable." My heart sank because I was loyal and worked hard for him. How can he say that? Where is the caring of a leader? That was my first reality lesson for the corporate world.

The business dream came back to me so I left the company and established a consultant company of my own. I was afraid because I never opened a consultant business before. My wife, Kim Phuong, and my two young children, at the age of 5 and 4, were also fearful because we had a mortgage and if we do not have enough income we would become homeless when the bank forecloses the house. I had many questions with no answers but I was able to convince my wife and pushed forward with the business. To my surprise, most of the clients followed me to my business. My brother and I started to learn how to manage a business on the fly. This is a very bad mistake for creating a business that has complexity such as a consulting business. We were fortunate enough to run into a friend who quickly helped us establish the proper papers for incorporation, setup services contracts, getting the business insurance, etc. The business took off and generated half a million annually for the last three years of the five years we were in business. Another mistake that we made was not managing our cash flow properly; we reinvested in unnecessary equipment and did not build our assets. With the business finances getting worse and my marriage about to crumble because of lacking a steady income for the family, I decided to put my business dream aside one more time; I returned to the corporate world again. This time I knew how it works and had learned a lot about human behavior, leadership, and relationship building. I got my project management certification. I have tried doing a side business as a life insurance salesman for about two years in network marketing arena. I had my life insurance license and was able to make some sales but this was not my passion. I am still in the corporate world but at the same time a business owner and an investor.

My life changed about four years ago when I met Khoa Le at the temple where I came regularly to develop my spiritual being. Khoa and I worked on a few charitable projects and I had the opportunity to get to know Khoa and his family better. At a young age, Khoa already had no intention of working for others and always wanted to be a business owner. Kim, his wife, had seen her family doing labor work for others for so many years; she felt the same way as her husband. Khoa has six years in the life insurance business and 15 years in the real estate investment business. His success came after he and

10

his wife almost became homeless overnight. Khoa established many companies after working for New York Life Company such as Akimax (a real estate company), First Design (an interior decoration staging), and Building Expo (a construction management company).

In late 2006 and with the marketing change for the down turn, Khoa found himself in a bind with financial challenges. He was not able to support the family; he was forced to foreclose most of his houses where he lost money. He was evicted from his home, his car was re-possessed. His family slept in the street for one night. With a helping hand from a friend, who is now an investor with our company, Khoa has rebuilt the company much stronger by applying what he had learned from many great coaches and business friends who are now millionaires. It took him 6 months to rebuild everything he lost. This is an indication of how experienced Khoa is in the field of real estate investment.

Chapter 1

The Journey Begins Within

"Strength does not come from physical capacity. It comes from an indomitable will."

Mahatma Gandhi

WHEN I WAS YOUNG MY PARENTS WERE VERY PROTECTIVE SO the seven of us never learned how to ride a bike. When living in Mexico, Missouri, I decided to learn how to ride a bike. The trouble is I only thought about learning and did not do anything about it. One day a friend of mine talked about doing a paper route to make money for a trip to Six Flags. The paper route requires you to have a bike. It triggered my need because I've never been to Six Flags and the desire to go there was high. Within one week I learned how to ride the bike and within a month I made enough money to go to Six Flags with my friends.

The above story demonstrates that when you have a clear reason why, a clear goal, and with enough determination, you will accomplish your dream. Did my friend do that for me? No. Did the newspaper company do it for me? No. I did it for myself and no one else. You see, the power is within you and it is ready to play its part whenever you allow it to flow.

I have been a smoker for the last 30 years and I have tried to quit many times because my children have asked me to. I was able to stop for a few months but then I started smoking again. With the recent events, I attended the enlightened warrior training camp from Peak Potentials. During this camp I discovered that if you stay focused, grounded, and committed to yourself, you would be able to overcome any obstacles that stand in your way. During the camp, the camp leader asked if any of the smokers are willing to stop smoking the 4 days of camp. I volunteered for the challenge. Somehow within the next day, I decided to quit smoking for good. Many of my teammates encouraged me for my effort and they believed in me. With that, I have been smoke-free ever since and still going strong. I am very proud of myself and every day I look at the cigarettes and say "I see you but I do not need you." And the whole day is a great smoke-free day.

Real estate investment is the same way. Once you get a lead, follow through with it and don't let it sit because it will slip away from you. I'd like to share with you a story about inner strength and the power of action.

There was a farmer who lived on a very lovely farm. He loves everything about his farm except for two things. One is an old wounded donkey and the other is a dried-up well, which he never did fill up. He tried to figure out how to get rid of these two things but could not find a good solution. One day the wounded donkey was walking about. He tripped on a big rock and fell into the well. The farmer did not see the donkey around the whole day so he was looking for it the next morning. He found it in the dried well and thought to himself, "This is great! I finally have the opportunity to clear the two ugliest things on this farm." The donkey on the other hand was struggling to climb out of the well. He was desperate and running out of hope. Suddenly he felt something hit his back and he realized that it was dirt that the owner was dumping on him. The first reaction was, "I am going to die from being buried alive by my owner." Just then, a thought came into his mind of how he can leverage the situation to survive. With that, he shook the dirt off his back every time the dirt landed on him. As the farmer continued dumping the dirt, the donkey continued shaking it off. Soon the donkey found himself near the edge of the well and he jumped out to safety. As you can see, everyone has the power to control the situation and manage the risk. The donkey let thoughts become his feelings, and he took action on his feelings, which led to the result he was looking for which is survival and freedom from the well. You have the power to learn, to identify risk, and to manage risk. That knowledge will remove fear from within you and give you the power to control your own investment outcome.

As I stepped into the career path of my life, I have learned from many successful people that you need to have a goal and vision. Your goals and visions must be clear and concise with an achievable time line. With that said, my goals were to be a successful manager where I lead many people and make a decent salary to support my family; I planned to reach this goal in about two years. This is a decent goal; however it does not have a strong motivation for me to reach a higher level of success. The reason why is because I don't have a strong desire to make it big with the previous goal. As mentioned before, I have created a business, successfully holding and growing the business for five years, and in the end I lost it. I spent a number of days in searching for the reason why I have failed in my business. After a long hard look, I discovered that I do not have a "big why."

What is a big why, you might ask? A big why is the primary reason you are dedicating your life to make it happen and to spend the results with loved ones. For me it is my wife, my children, and my parents. I want to make a lot of money so that I can have the time to spend with my family. I would like to be able to help anyone at any given time and not worry about financial capabilities.

I was searching for my "why" for over two years until the day I attended the Millionaire Mind Intensive and it triggered my deepest emotions and at that moment I found my "why" – the reason I am thriving to do better, to be better, and to accomplish more. They are my children. I've been living with the mindset of staying within my comfort zone and being satisfied with what I have. I never thought of wanting more or living my life fuller. The lesson was the most fearful thought that has plagued me for a long time. The answer was the fear of not being able to give the best to my children, the fear of not giving them the knowledge they need to achieve their dreams, and the fear of having my children living below a certain lifestyle. They deserved more. My wife deserved more. I wanted to leave a legacy for my children, grandchildren, and great-grandchildren. This is the motivation I needed to find the purpose within, the strength, the mental toughness I needed to be successful.

As you can see, it is critical to have a motive to drive you forward to reach your destiny. I would ask at this point in time that you would stop reading and spend some time thinking about what is your big why.

Here is a bonus for you. Once you have completed your big why, please go to our website at http://www.reiinvest.com and share your big why with me by sending an email though "contact us." In return, you will receive one free week of access to our construction estimating tool. It's a tool that everyone who is doing property rehab definitely needs. It provides the best estimate of your construction cost. The tool gives you the leverage to negotiate for the best construction deals. Register with us to get your user name and password to our Construction Tools system.

As I mentioned from my business days above, the reason why I failed the business was because I did know how to manage my finances. For many years I have heard that one must have one's financial plan in place, but I was ignorant and did not follow through with educating myself in the matter. Over the period of 10 years, I was a millionaire but I do not have much to set aside for saving. I talked with many of my friends who were at the same level as I was and they were in the same position as me. They made a lot of money but were not able to retain much for saving and for retiring. Most of my friends put aside about 2% to 4% for their retirement plan and they would put very little effort in monitoring their retirement program.

About four years ago when I joined Primerica, I first heard the phrase, "Pay yourself first." The concept was foreign to me and I did not pay much attention to it. I continued to work hard and bring more money back to the family to spend. Yes, to spend and not to save. I was acquainted with many successful people who are millionaires or who would be millionaires. However I was not motivated to move forward. I got my life insurance license within 30 days of joining Primerica and I was making money within the next 60 days. I built a good team and even made it to Team Captain for three months. I found my motivation decreasing daily and I continued to procrastinate. I did not quit but I did not do much either.

One day I saw a video on YouTube that talked about how everyone is a millionaire but never noticed. It was a simple calculation. If you make 60,000 a year and work for 20 years, you would have 1,200,000 (1.2 million). Wouldn't that qualify you as a millionaire? It certainly would. The question is where did my money go? Why do I not have any money saved? The answer is rather simple. It is because we do not have a plan. We do not know where we are with our financial situation. We are clueless about our income and spending.

I shared the information with my wife and we decided to take action to see how bad of a financial hole we are in by doing the following steps:

1. We filled out a family budget with some actual and some estimated amounts we knew of.

2. We monitored our income and spending for a few months to get closer to the actual amounts as we can.

3. We highlighted the spending that we thought was not beneficial to us and could be eliminated without changing our life style.

4. We had a family meeting and shared what we found with our children so that they understood our financial situation.

Knowing this will help them understand the tradeoff and that they need to keep only the best.

5. We continued keeping an eye on the budget.

6. We identified other sources of income that we could bring in.

Once we established the above system for the family, we began to set aside money for our savings. As I mentioned above, "paying yourselves first" is pertaining to answering one question: "If you do not exist, would you be able to make the money you are making today?" The answer would obviously be "no." If "no" is the answer then why wouldn't you pay yourselves first before paying to others such as the IRS, the credit cards, mortgage, etc... Paying yourselves first does not mean to neglect other debts but rather understanding what is more important in life for you.

Here is another lesson I learned about saving. The approach is to set aside 5 jars and put into each jar a percentage of your income every time you receive an income regardless of how big or small. The purpose here is to establish a habit and not how much of a percent you can save. With that said, you can start with any percentage you like. It is recommended to begin with 10% if you can. As for the 5 jars, they each have a name and a purpose. They are:

1. **Investment** – For money you set aside for investment. You put 10% of your income into this jar.

2. **Long-term Savings** – For vacations, a new car, or your children's education. You put 10% of your income into this jar.

3. **Personal Education** – Money to continue your own education because knowledge is money and knowledge removes fear from your mind. 10% of your income goes in here.

4. **Fun** – For celebrating your success because it gives you the motivation to do more and to accomplish more. 10% goes in this

jar. There is one caveat to this jar and you MUST use this every single month. You can take the family out to dinner; see a movie, or anything that your heart desires. The main thing is you MUST enjoy.

5. **Giving** – For money to give to a good cause. You can donate to your temple or church, buy some food for the homeless, give to your favorite charity organization, buy a gift for a needy child, or buy some flowers for the elderly in a nursing home, etc. These are just a few examples and you can do much more with this jar so let your imagination run wild. 5% goes into this jar.

Since I started practicing this, I have saved enough money to attend three large events of Peaks Potentials, two JT Foxx events, and was able to give three times more than I have given before to good causes. I also discovered that giving is a joyful event and I felt happy every time I gave. It is a wonderful feeling.

I strongly recommend you start discovering where you're at and where you want to be in your financial goals. Once you begin, the momentum will build up and you will find yourselves happy and anxious to do this on a daily basis.

Did you know that your worst enemy is yourself? Yes, you heard me correctly. A few of us have overcome ourselves and became millionaires and most of us are still in denial that we failed because of the people around us, because of the situation that we are in, or we are just not lucky enough to make it to the finish line. All of these are just excuses that we use to make ourselves feel better. Here is a quick test for you to validate what I am talking about. The test has only three questions and if you answer "yes" to all three questions then you are now closer to the truth and it is up to you to decide which way to be "better" or "worse."

Here are the three questions

1. Have you ever had a dream?

2. Do you have challenges in making your dream come true?

3. Have you given up on your dream?

Growing up you have heard many times your parents say "no" to you. Yes? They say "no" do not climb on the table you will hurt yourself, or "no" you cannot have a second soda, and many more "no's." However, as a child, did you give up or did you continue to nag and continue asking to have what you want? My children nag and nag and nag until I give in and give them what they want. What happened to that persistence that we had? As we grow older we allow the fear to overcome our thinking, which allows us to give up quickly.

When I was working with Primerica as a life insurance salesperson, I learned how weak I was. I often made excuses for my failures. I blamed my wife and family for my unsuccessfulness, which was wrong because it was me who failed. Recently I went on a training camp called Enlightened Warrior Training Camp. I learned that I have the power to overcome anything that comes my way because the definition of a warrior is "one who conquers oneself." As a warrior I will never give up. During this training camp I decided to stop smoking and, with mental determination, I have been smoke-free for 30 days as I write this book.

As you begin doing your real estate investing, having mental toughness is critical and a saying that has been keeping me going up until now is, "You can quit any time, but now is not the time."

Chapter 2

Knowing the Rules of the Game

KNOWING THE RULES OF THE GAME IS HALF THE BATTLE IN ANY situation or position. During my earlier experiences, as I mentioned above, I started a business without knowing the rules of the game. If I had known the rules, I could have saved my original business and avoided all the taxes and debts.

When I left my first job to open my first software services business, where did I get the customers for my business? They came from the relationships that I had built over time. Back then I did not even pay attention to the term "relationship" but I acted on it and in return I had many happy customers who were willing to follow me to my own consulting businesses.

Even in my corporate career, many of my managers and mentors mentioned to me that I need to be visible and focus on establishing the relationships with other departments because it is a lever that will help you move up in the corporate ladder. As I begin to study this development opportunity I discovered that by building a relationship with others, you allow yourself to be seen by others for who you are. It can be good or bad but it's an opportunity to discover oneself and opportunity to change your brand. Your success or failure depends on your brand. In addition, I also learned that relationships allow you to see other mistakes so that you can learn from them and avoid the errors that could cost you dearly.

Building relationships is also a cultural behavior. For Asian people, most of them are quiet, like to stay behind the scenes, and not likely to volunteer for the main role. This is obviously different from the Western world. It is also a personality behavior as well. There are people who can make connections so naturally while those like me don't find it so easy. It took me some time to change my behavior and once I changed, it became the most powerful tool for me. Now I can interact with others, learn what they do, find opportunities to help them, and ask others for help if I need it. As a wise man said, "building relationships is like building a financial bank."

To demonstrate my point about giving, I would like to share with you a story. We live in a universe with an abundance of gifts. If we are willing to give unconditionally, we will receive gifts from the universe, which are often much more than what we have given. May I share with you a story I have read from the internet? This story triggered my thinking about giving.

A boy named Lula was born in October 1945 to a farming family in West Babylon (Brazil). For being poor, at the age of four, the boy had to sell peanuts on the streets with ragged clothes and often not enough food to eat. After he got into middle school, Lula moved to the capital, Rio de Janeiro, along with two friends. They shined shoes at the street corner after school, to make some money to help the family. They would starve for the day if they did not get any customers.

One afternoon, when Lula was 12, the owner of a nearby dry clean store gave the boys a chance to shine his shoes. The three boys ran to the customer and waited to see which one would take the offer. The man looked at the boys' earnestly begging eyes and he could not decide who would shine his shoes. Finally he said, "Whoever needs the money the most will shine my shoes and I will give them two coins."

The service fee is only 20 cents and two coins is a large amount to have. The three boys' eyes lit up. One boy said, "I have not eaten since this morning. If I do not make any money I would be starved today." Another boy said, "We ran out of food three days ago, my mom is sick, and I must get some food for the family tonight, otherwise I will be punished."

Lula looked at the two coins in the hands of the customer and thought for a moment then said, "If I could earn these two coins from you today, I would give my friends one coin each." Lula's statement completely and utterly surprised the customer and his two friends. He slowly explained, "They are my best friends, they have not eaten all day long, and I ate some peanuts during lunch. I would then be the best person to shine your shoes and you would be very satisfied with my work." Touched by the boy's statement, the customer paid two silver coins after Lula had finished polishing his shoes. Holding true to his promise, Lula immediately gave each friend one coin.

A few days later, the business owner came looking for Lula and accepted him as the apprentice to his dry cleaning business where dinner was included with the apprentice job. The wage is very low but it is much better in comparison to shoe shining after school. Lula understood that because he had given a helping hand to those that are more in need, he was given an opportunity that changed his life.

Since then, whenever he had a chance, Lula did not hesitate in helping more people that are less fortunate. Later, Lula quit school to work for a factory. There he defended the rights of the workers by joining the union group. At 45, Lula founded the Workers' Party.

In 2002, Lula's slogan for his presidency campaign is, "There will be three full meals for everyone in this country" and Lula became the president of Brazil. For the full eight years in office, he kept his promise: 93 % of children and 83 % of adults in his country are living in prosperity.

The power of giving is very strong. With the right mindset, you could begin by helping a few and those few will grow into larger numbers, leading to opportunities that you would not expect, as Lula had experienced. This is true with many successful business owners such as Donald Trump, Steve Jobs, Bill Gates, Warren Buffett, etc.

If you have not begun opening your heart, I strongly encourage you to start. Lending a helping hand does not mean you must give money. You can begin by spending the time to listen to a friend in need, give quick advice, and/or just being there as a friend. You can also leverage the giving and saving which I spoke of in chapter 1 above.

"We make a living by what we get. We make a life by what we give."

Winston Churchill

We have talked about establishing one's relationship capital because it will lead to financial capital. How do we begin? Where do we get connections from? How do we maintain the connection? These are all great questions and knowing the answers will bring you closer to the winning finish line.

You might have heard the saying, "It is not who you know but who knows you" or "It is better for others to promote you than you promoting yourself."

Being you is important but being you in the spot light is even more important because you allow people to see you for you. With an open mind, you allow people to know you better, know your abilities, your strengths and weaknesses, and with an open mind you also begin to learn about others around you and how you can connect with them.

You can get connection anywhere. I don't think finding out where is important but the better question to ask is "Are you willing to be uncomfortable in getting to know other people?" If you are not willing to reach out then it does not matter where. Here is an exercise you can do every morning to overcome the shyness. After the normal hygiene tasks are done, close your eyes and say to yourself "I am an interesting person to know", "How are you today <your name>?", and "I am going to speak to three new people today." Talk to the people about themselves, their family, and their interests. These are topics most commonly used to strike a conversation. Once you are able to begin a simple conversation, churches, temples, seminars, community events, and charitable events are the best places to get to know more people. You can begin practicing in a familiar environment such as churches and temples.

One thing you might want to pay attention to is, to get better, you need to hang out with people who are more successful than you because you can learn from them by observing how they talk, how they dress, and how they genuinely care or listen to the people they meet. These realistic lessons will change the way you think, act, and get results.

In looking back at my first investment meeting a few years back I could not avoid a smile on my face because I was so horrible at the time. It was a Friday night and the meeting was with my sister and her boyfriend in Livermore. As I drove out to her house, I was practicing all the right sentences to say or not to say. I was not at all confident in my knowledge. I came to her house 10 minutes earlier then the appointment time so I waited in the car and reviewed even more information to share with her. I started out chitchatting about her job, the children, the dogs, and so on. This is the fundamental in a sales pitch. When we got into the conversation, she began to ask me questions which I was not prepared to answer because I just do not have the information. So I took the questions down and I was glad that it was my sister that I was talking to. The lessons learned here are:

1. Anticipate the unexpected questions and prepare to answer them.

2. Know the story not the facts.

3. Speak from the heart even though you are not closing the deal.

Anticipating questions like "how will you be able to secure my money?" "With the market nowadays how can you give the return you indicated?" or "What type of investment are you in?" "Is this like stock?" etc.

Presenting the answers in a story like manner will trigger more the client's emotional feeling about joining because "facts tell and stories sell". In addition, when you speak from the heart, people will know and they will see that you care for their own benefits which will increase their trust in you. They might not do business with you right then and there but they will do business with you because of your integrity.

Here is a story to take my point home. One day a couple came to my office and they brought with them a binder of papers. They sat down and we started to talk and they told me about their situation. The husband is working and he had two previous 401K accounts that have been rolled over with another company recently. The wife is a homemaker and they had some cash to invest and that money was also with another company. They are not making money but they are not losing money. If they transfer over to our company they would earn 4% to 8% interest from our company. In further talking with the couple and in looking at the contract, they would lose 3% penalty for early termination and would also lose the 5% bonus they received as a promotion. In reviewing the situation, the loss is much greater than the gain if they switch. I told them it would not be in their best interest to switch over to our company right now. They were surprised at the recommendation that I made and told me that they admire us for being honest. Two weeks later, another couple came to us and opened an account with us and guess what? They were referred by the previous couple. That proves to me that if you are honest and treat others well, you will reap greater benefits.

Here are two things that I always do to get new prospects and/or convert them into clients:

1. Here is a question/script for getting an appointment with a warm or cold market. "If I can show you a way to earn more return on an investment that is much more stable than stock market, would you be interested?" If yes, schedule an appointment right then and there.

2. During the appointment, you need to ask the prospect the question, "Why do you want to invest?" Based on the answer, you need to tell the potential client two things – the consequences for investing and the consequences for not investing.

This technique has worked for me and has given me the confidence and opportunity to convert prospects into customers.

Chapter 3

The Hunt for Properties

N THIS CHAPTER I THOUGHT I WOULD CHANGE THE METHOD A BIT to make it more interactive. I will provide the information in the form of an interview where I asked actual people in our organization who manage a particular area of the system. This approach provides you insight to the person and the role the person has and how it would enable or hinder the process. It will help you be successful and help you to prevent delays in your project.

Before I start I would like to take this moment to share with you that our trustee system is a unique system that can be applicable in any county in any of the 50 states. If you visit our company website at www.reiinvest.com and register with our company, you will get a one week free trail of our Trustee Sales system. This is one of the four fabulous bonuses that we promise to you. Visit www.reiinvest.com to gain access to this incredible tool.

During a good market where the banks are releasing large quantities of homes for auction, we leverage the trustee sales system we developed to acquire the properties. However, during a slow market, the banks are holding the properties and we would have to approach the process differently. The following chapters will include conversations I had with our special team who have mastered the trustee auction process. Let the interview begin.

Khoa Le is the founder and co-owner of REI Invest Inc. He has over 15 years of real estate investment experience and specializes in the auction area.

Question (Q): In this market where there are not many houses to buy, how do you get the properties you are getting?

35

Answer (A): This is a good question and may I answer this with a short story? We came from a business environment where my great-grandfather was a businessman, as were my grandfather, my father, etc. In short, we have done business for many generations. I remember when we first came to America we worked for someone else for exactly three months before we opened our first business, which was a phone card company. I had no clue about the business so I started to look for people who had done this before and learned from them. I treated them well by compensating them for their time. In treating people fairly, I have gained much respect and trust from the people around me from vendors to customers. I connected with many distributors and slowly got connected to the source. After 6 to 8 months, I had completely organized, opened and fully operated my own Phone Card Business system. The point to this story is that you need to evaluate people for their people skills, communication skills, and most of all, be enthusiastic about selling. I leverage the above approach to connect to a few trusted agents, adjusters, and appraisers who help me look for properties that are in pre-foreclosure, bank owned, or being sold by owner. Let's call all of them "agents" for ease of our conversation. The agents are on the road most of the time or they have been around the neighborhood so the people around the properties felt comfortable and they are happy to provide information as needed.

(Q): Would you be selective in choosing people for your team? What criteria would you be looking for?

(A): Yes, I must be selective when choosing people for my team. If you do not have the right people with the appropriate skills you would end up doing everything yourselves and never get anything done. I am looking for people with passion for what they do. Have you seen a football player or players in any sports that became famous and listen to what they said about their career in the beginning? The answers are always "Play from the heart and with the love for the game." In real estate investment it is the same. This is the reason I am looking for people with love for the business.

(Q): Where would you be looking for properties?

(A): The simple answer is through network connections. We asked our agents, our friends to connect us with foreclosed homes that they know of, with Real Estate Owned (REO) agents that have properties to push out into the market, most of the time we ask our people to pay attention to the properties that they see in the street. The last method is the best way because you can pick and choose. The criteria selections are 1) The neighborhood condition, 2) The property condition, and 3) Schools and businesses around the area. If the property meets two of the three criteria we get the address of the properties and begin our process.

Summary: Before acquiring the right properties, we must first choose the right team of people who are passionate and love what they do. These qualities will help the team identify good potential properties to acquire. In other words, hunting for properties is an easy process but hunting for the hunters is a bigger challenge. As the business owner, be respectful, be fair, and be loyal to your people because they are your biggest assets.

You hear the saying, "location, location, location" a lot in real estate. Yes, it is true that location is important to the value of the properties but it is not the most critical criteria to look at. In this section, we would like to focus on not the location itself but how a person who is investing can look at demographic in order to make a decision in purchasing the properties.

(Q): In the beginning of your career, what was the biggest challenge that you had in learning about real estate investments?

(A): The biggest challenge I would say is remembering all the aspects of an area by zip code. You cannot do this overnight so be patient and learn as you go. I started my real estate business in 2005. Since I always pay close attention to everything around me, I began to notice things like how far the schools are in a particular area, the school names, how many of them are high schools or elementary schools, how far the nearest supermarket is, if there are any other types of markets in the area, and so on. As you can see this information is important to a buyer's decision.

(Q): What is the best approach in learning the demographic based on your experiences?

(A): The best approach is learning by doing. I started out by having a pocket-sized notebook. I wrote down the zip code in the notebook, gave the zip code a few pages (4 to 5), and I started to record the information. Whenever I drive around the area I pay attention to schools, super markets, parks, businesses, etc. I make the effort to stop and ask the people who live there about the area. I then write down the information into my note book afterward. Be advised, do not write notes while talking to people because they might not like it and they might not be willing to share more information. Another approach is asking people who already have knowledge in that area such as your own real estate agents network. Take them out to lunch and pick their brain.

(Q): Are there any other resources that would help you build up your demographic knowledge?

(A): Yes and they are local seminars, librarians, media, etc. You can tap into these areas to learn more about the demographic details because they will give different viewpoints, particularly from the common people who live there in regard to crime rates, friendliness of the people, and ethnicity perspective.

Summary: The demographic lesson is focused on techniques in knowing an area and most important is to develop a consistent behavior that could get you the most details about an area. With that you will appear confident and knowledgeable in your field. The most important point here to me is "action." You can read all you can but if you do not put any in practice you will not learn anything at all.

- Get a pocket size notebook to capture zip code demographic details.

- Notice and write down the information about the zip code.

- Ask people who live in the area.

- Ask your network of friends who already know the details.

- Review and repeat the details to memorize them.

In purchasing the properties for investment, the key lesson is getting the property with the lowest value possible because it is the biggest profit in your investment. The questions I often get are:

1. Where do I go to get the most accurate pricing?

2. How do I find what the comparable values in the area are?

3. How can I tell if the price I get is the lowest?

As a beginner investor, you need to learn how to get the pricing yourself but as you get to be move advanced, let other people do the work for you so that you can spend your time with more strategic tasks.

As property comes to you either by you knowing the property or by other people providing you the lead, getting the property's comparable prices should be the very first task you need to complete. This will give you the foundation of the property and you build from there. The most accurate site is MLS (www.mls.com) or MLS Listing (www.mlslisting.com) but you must be a real estate agent to have access to these two web sites. There are costs associated with these two web sites. If you have a chance to become a real estate agent and you desire to become one then that's great. What I am saying is that you do not have to be a real estate agent to do this. This addressed question number 1 above.

With the property address, you can get onto Zillow (www.zillow.com) or Trulia (www.trulia.com) to find the information you need about the property. The details you need to pay attention to are:

- The asking prices
- The property information (square footage, number of beds, etc.)
- Year built

First look at the information above to get a feeling about the property. Then you would look at the properties surrounding the property you're about to purchase. At this point compare the square footage, number of rooms, garage, or other information such as a pool, etc. Most of this information is already there on the web sites mentioned above for you to look into.

I can show you all the techniques but I cannot show you the emotions and feelings when you're researching the property because each of our emotions is different. Your emotions will be different from the buyer's. Knowing the market value and the buyer's emotions will allow you to evaluate and set the proper listing price, which will give you the highest profit. This addressed question number 2 above.

After you have looked into the property details, now it is time to pay attention to the other information such as who is doing the listing, how long has it been on the list, how is the rating for the area the property is in, etc. Why do we need to know this? It is because it will determine what value you would offer on the property. It gives you the leverage for negotiation.

We had a property in the Stockton area and it is a fourplex. The property is in an average neighborhood. The property was built back in the 50's so the sewer system is not the best and with regulation changes, the sewer system is one of the issues we need to resolve. Knowing this information we can work with the seller to lower the price of the property which we did. This negotiation adds the values to our profit up front as I mentioned in the beginning of this section.

Now that you have found out about the existing price, you're able to lower the buying values. Did this give you the information of how much you would profit from the property yet? The answer is "no" not yet. What other pieces of information are you missing? It is the future market value. Knowing what the market value has been around the property in the past or current will give the insight to how much profit you would get.

Let's go back to the example above. Looking at the selling history for the property in Stockton, we know that similar properties have been sold at $300,000 a few years back and at the current some similar properties have been sold at $280,000. The asking price is at $225,000 and with the information we had about the sewer system, we have put in an offer at $175,000 where we would inform the seller about the sewer system issue, how much it would cost to fix the issue, and how long it would take to have the project complete. If the seller is not selling the property now, the value of the property will go down as time passes. After the negotiation, we bought the property at $180,000 which gives us a gap of $120,000 profit.

With the demonstration above, do you see the importance of knowing the pricing in this game? I hope you did. This address question number 3 above.

Summary: We summarize this process for you to ease the learning process.

- The objective is buying the property with the lowest price possible.
- Get the property address and use Zillow or Trulia to learn about:
  - The asking price
  - The price of at least three nearby properties with similar square footage and criteria
  - Property details
- Doing comparable research.
- Asking for history selling prices from your network.
- Determine the profit gap with future selling price minus the buying price.
- Prepare and know the information before heading into the offer process.

To be effective in property rehab is to have the funds at hand because there is no time for loan process and, in all cases, paying in full via a cashier's check is required for the trustee sales process. We have heard about private lending but what is it and how does it work?

Private lending is money from personal assets being loaned to start up a business or for any purpose. In our case it is for buying real estate, in short term with a percentage that is normally higher than banks. Investors with cash assets can lend you the money and they act as a bank. The interest rate depends on the loan amount and the term of the loan. Small amounts in a short term will most likely have smaller rates of return.

Here is my conversation with my partner Khoa in perspective of presenting the information in this book.

(Q): In your opinion, is private lending a good way to gain capital for your project and/or business?

(A): Private lending is a method to gain capital and to me it is just a way to raise funds. I would advise startup businesses to approach investors using self-directed IRA first because it is less risky and investors' money is protected by the trust companies.

(Q): How would you approach someone about investing money with you or be your private lender?

(A): As you know, all deals are made with trust between two parties. Establishing trust is critical in the fund-raising process. My experience taught me to 1) build your brand via marketing, 2) let people know who you are, what you do, and what benefits the investors will get, 3) giving back to the community.

1. Building your brand via advertisement with the local media (newspaper, radio, and television). It also depends on your target audience in order for this to be effective for you. If you have not defined your target audience, please set aside time to do this because it will lead you to your investors the fastest.

2. In the age of information technology, we have many tools that can help us connect with many people at one time. They are called websites, social networks, and mass mailing. Find a way to tab into these resources to bring your name and your business name to the public.

3. Both you and I are passionate about giving back because giving is the most rewarding experience for us every time we complete an event. You have done this much more than I have in this area however for the point that we are trying to share is that by doing charitable works, helping the community, and giving back to the community will definitely bring your name and your business name closer to the people in your area. You build trust with your potential investors.

What I have shared above has nothing to do with private lending but it has everything to do with raising the funds you need to buy, fix, and sell homes. I strongly recommend you look into this before beginning the rehab business. In regards to approaching people, you start with your warm market which are your close friends, relatives, and people that already trust you. They can be your promoters as soon as they see the benefits. Next you would have a small team doing cold calling for you to setup appointments. During the appointment you would clarify and answer all the questions which will lead to a closing by signing the contract. Here are a few things you want to pay attention to during the conversation with the investors.

1. Believe in your products but do not pressure the investors to lend you the money during the presentation. . Remember that trust is a factor.

2. Tell the investors success stories from other investors.

3. Just be their friends and be there for them. They will come to you when they are ready.

Summary: If you have not done any private lending before, you should leverage the knowledge of someone who has done it before. The concept is to communicate to the investors that being a bank is the best passive income they can ever make. Leverage technologies to get your name to many people to build your brand. First start with your warm market and ask them for testimonials to gain more investors. For cold calling, here is a script that we used to setup appointments with potential investors: "If we can show you how to get the most return on investment where it is more stabilized than the stock market, would you be interested?" If the answer is yes, lock in the date and time for the appointment.

Chapter 4

Make It Fun

WE HAVE A TRUSTEE SYSTEM THAT ALLOWS YOU TO TRACK auction properties which we need to do the research on so that we can intelligently bid on the properties. Inspecting the property is one of the steps in our process. Knowing what the property looks like, the condition it is in, and the neighborhood will help the system in determining if the property is a good buy or not.

Bang is our field inspector specialist. He has been doing this for the last 5 years. His story will help us understand the inspection process and how important it is.

(Q): Can you tell us in general what your job is and how important it is to the buying process?

(A): My primary job is to gather everything there is to know about the property so that the next team can do their job. If the information I provide is not accurate then the outcome will cause tremendous consequences for the business because the details I provide enable the decision making of buying or not buying the property.

(Q): Can you walk us through your inspection process?

(A): My inspection must be completed prior to the auction date. This means if the auction is tomorrow then my inspection tasks must be done today. My inspection is based on a point system where the house inspection point plus the point of construction needed yield a result which feed into the next step in decision making. Here is my typical day:

My day begins at 6 AM where I would turn on my equipment which includes my desktop computer, my laptop, and my iPad. I review my list of properties that need inspection. I exclude all canceled and postponed properties from my list and only focus on the auction listing which is about 10 to 15 properties a day. These properties are new to me so to make the best use of my time, I look at them one by one using Google Earth, Zillow, and Map Quest because I need to know what the properties look like, where they are located so that I do not waste time searching for the properties and plan my driving route based on the properties' address and zip code. I normally open as many websites as I can so that I can determine the following information

1. Is this a single home, condominium, townhouse, or apartment?

2. If it is single family home, how may stories does it have?

3. How does the property look in Zillow and Google Earth?

4. What are the street names and what part of the city is it in?

The benefits of the above information are 1) you have a travel plan that helps you minimize the driving time (gas saving), 2) avoid traffic time, and 3) manage your time. This process is the most time consuming and normally takes about 3 to 4 hours. Once we have the list of properties the next step is to drive to each address to gather the information. Since we are given a particular set of zip codes, we focus only in that zip code. Since we are doing the inspection in advance, we must complete everything by 6 PM.

(Q): The process you mentioned seems to be complicated but essential in determining to buy or not. Can you share with me what are the normal activities once you reached the property?

(A): With the basic information prepared, the next step is physically viewing the property. This is a technique in itself because you are about to convey the information by words so that the owner can visualize the property, knowing the neighborhood. This requires great communication skill with precision. To be accurate in my description I would report the following:

1. The neighborhood – Is it a good neighbor and how can you determine if it is good or bad? For example – Normally you see two cars can be parked on the house drive way. You come to a neighbor where you see that there are three or four cars parked that blocked the side walk and even parked on the lawn. If you see many cases like this in the part of town your property is in, would you think this is a good or not so good? It would be not so good because it is crowded and could cause issue with the parking.

2. The property at 360 degrees – You need to pay attention to the roof, the windows, the lawn, etc. which I will come back to later.

Summary: To properly determine the value of the house, inspection is needed and a good inspector will take pride in his work. He will be committed to get the job done and have a system and plan for his daily activities. His diligence is a big contribution to the company's success. Key points are:

- Clearly document the finding.

- Learn how to paint the picture with words.

- Complete the task in the same day.

- Leverage technologies to get a 360 degree view.

- Learn to pay attention to details.

(Q): Can you go into details on what would you be looking for from the property?

(A): The critical items that you need to pay attention to are anything that are related to 1) the beauty of the property and 2) the safety of the property.

With that said, you need to inspect the roof next. There are many types of roofs such as shingle combo roof, wooden roof, red tile roof, gray tile roof, marble roof, etc. You **must** be clear in stating the type of roofing and the condition. Is it difficult to tell if there are any damages to the roof when it looks decent because the wooden roofing looks brand new? Yes it is difficult however you can always tell. Here is an example. If the roof is wooden roofing, look to see if they're bending in any way or not. If yes, it is an indication the roof is leaking.

Next you look at the gutter to see if it's straight or bent. This will give you the indication of water damage from within the wall. This will lead to molding and the repair cost can be high. Based on my experience, if the outside is not being taken care of, the inside is most likely to be the same.

You should also pay attention to windows. Look to see if the window is single or double pane. The majority of the houses were built in the 60's and 70's. Back then, double pane windows were not available. If the owner did not replace the windows to double pane, the house is prone for repair from within as well. Would you think an owner would replace the inside furnishings to save money without changing the windows? I would say no. It does not make sense.

The garage door is also important because it is a safety issue if the garage door is not being updated to meet the city code. An older type of garage can be faulty and does not have the sensor to prevent accidents especially with small children.

Next I would look at the exterior of the property such as paint, window trimming, and the paint color. Some of the properties have a fresh new coat of paint but the color is not appropriate with the buyer's market. The color might be good for a few people but it is not for the majority. Paint cost will then need to be added to the fix up cost so that we can recover when we sell the property. Besides the painting, one should also notice the decor of the exterior of the house. Exterior design increases the property values.

Landscape plays a critical role as well. Inspecting the landscape will also determine if the house value goes up or down. If the lawn is dry and looks like it has not been maintained for a while then it is an indication that the owner does not care much or the sprinkler system is not working.

There might be times when we can easily overlook the obvious. If there is a tree with one part no longer visible, the inspector will not see that the missing part of the tree has fallen and pressed on the roof if he is not observant. This type of damage is equivalent to a burned down home because you will need city permits to fix the problem. This will lead to delays in selling the property due to the slowness of the local city planning department.

Let me circle back to the roof again because it is important to avoid a law suit at a later time. Make sure you look underneath the roofing because if the house was damaged by fire the evidence is most likely to show up there and the owner often forgets to fix that area. Even if it was fixed, you can also see the fire evidence if you look carefully.

(Q): You have demonstrated that you carefully inspect the property both outside and inside. Besides the critical criteria in the above question, do you look for moisture in areas? How can you spot them?

(A): Moisture or water leak on the ground is important but it is not as important if there is moisture on the wall. If you look carefully you will see that the moisture makes the paint color slightly darker than the rest of the dry wall section. This shows that there were leaks in the property. This type of leakage mostly happens in the garage because the garage is connected to the main property housing body and there are often hairline cracks there so we must be careful during the inspection time.

(Q): Some properties are located in the middle of the block where you can see clearly the front view and a partial view on left/right side, but you are not able to see the back. In this situation, what would you do to be able to see a complete view?

(A): With Google Earth 3D you can see the properties on the three sides but, to be honest with you, if you see the front of the house as I have described above, you can guess what the back of the house looks like.

(Q): Earlier you mentioned that the inspection is on a point system. Could you provide more on how it works and how it can impact the decision making process?

(A): When we stand in front of the house, we should be able to see that the roof is okay, the garage door is in good condition, and there is good lighting in the front of the house. It should also have double-pane windows, a beautiful design, and the paint should be good. Let's use a human face as an example. If you look at a person that has great eyes, clean haircut, and smooth skin, you can probably assume that person takes good care of themselves and also assume that the rest of the body would be in the same condition. If you see a person with messy hair, how would you feel about that person? You would probably not give it much credit, yes? Same thing applies with the house. The front of the house is like a person's hairdo. If it is not clean then the rest of the house would not be clean. The point system is the popularity measuring of the house, how much fixing up it would need. Based on this judgment, here's how I grade the house:

- 9 – 10 are for brand new houses. This is extremely rare to come by for foreclosure and auctioning.

- 8 – 8.99 are for houses in perfect condition. We have a few of these and they are often up on the hills or nearby country clubs.

- 7 – 7.99 are houses in great condition. These are upper end houses. During the good seller market, you will not see much of these houses.

- 6 – Below are houses in fair condition. These are more common because of the neighborhood.

We start out with an overall score of points then we move in to the details. As we see things that need fixing, we would deduct points from the base score. At the end, you would then provide estimation for construction. The amount spent is just to bring the house back to its base point. If you want a higher score, then you would need to increase the construction cost. Here is an example: Let's say the property base score is 7 and you discovered the roof and three other areas need fixing. You deduct half a point, bringing the score to 6.5. With the estimation of $15,000 in fixing-up costs, it would bring the score back to 7. The next step would be to evaluate the nearby properties and the condition that they are in to determine how to maintain the property that you own. If they are not then why should we spend the money? In this case I would mark the house as "backup" and leave the final decision to the auctioneer to decide at the bidding time.

(Q): I am not clear on the term "backup" you stated. Would you care to clarify?

(A): It means if you have better properties to bid on then take it. If, on that day, there are no properties to buy, the bidding is safe and low value, so then we should bid on backup houses. In another words, they are our second choices of properties to buy if the bidding value is low.

Summary: Looking at the issue and identifying it greatly contribute to the decision of acquiring the property or not, what the offer price would be, and what is the maximum amount we are willing to accept. The most important is the water damage to the interior of the property. The more accurate your report is, the more accurate the estimate of the repair cost will be, and that can save the company a lot of headache down the line.

- Pay attention to the roof.
- Look for evidence of fire damage.
- Provide a scoring point and estimated construction cost.
- Document the note clearly and accurately.

(Q): When inspecting, is the way you dress important and could it cause some concern with the neighbors?

(A): Yes, it is important. You should not wear shorts or t-shirts and make sure to tuck in your shirt. You should be well-dressed and professional-looking. As you know, we are being judged every day for everything we do from dressing to walking. A well-dressed person would not raise any concerns. On the other hand, if you dress in shorts or look unprofessional then the people would be suspicious about what you are up to. The objective is to be inconspicuous; the less attention you draw to yourselves the better.

(Q): Do you stay in the car or walk around when you're inspecting the house?

(A): It depends if the area is safe or not. Most of the time I walk around for a closer look and some of the time you can see pretty well inside your car. I often inspect corner houses from my car. Additionally, Google Earth usually provides some evidence already and there is sometimes no need for walking around.

(Q): Have you run into situations where the neighbors or owner come up and threaten you? If yes, how did you handle the situation?

(A): Yes, there were incidents where they came up to me and threatened to call the police on me. In those situations, I strongly recommended them to contact the police but told them I would only give the police 5 minutes to arrive before I leave. A few had called but the police did not come within 5 minutes so I left.

The inspector needs to understand the emotions that the owner is feeling when their house is being short-sold or foreclosed. They are about to lose a big part of their livelihood so understanding this would help you tremendously in dealing with angry owners. On the other hand, we would also make clear to them in a respectful way that we aware of the law and need to take precautions to protect ourselves, such as:

1. In some cases, the owner seems to be very friendly and invites you in to look at the inside of the house. You would respectfully decline the invitation and **under no circumstances should you enter the property** because once you enter the property you will be liable for trespassing or forced entry even though you did not.

2. When being questioned why you are looking at the house, you need to calmly explain that you cannot share the information because you are just doing your job. Sometimes they think you are bank personnel and you are here to make the case worse for them.

3. In case you need to take pictures, please make sure that you have the owner's or tenant's permission before doing so.

4. When the owner or tenant approaches you, you need to stay calm, treat them with respect and don't treat them as if you are better than them in any way. Pay attention to their emotional state because it will give insight to their behavior and help you turn the situation around.

5. Never get into a confrontation with the owners or tenants. The best thing is to walk away. You can come back at a later time to finish up your work.

6. There are times they will come to your car and try to break your car windows. In this case carefully move away.

After providing his answers, Bang turned and asked me for my opinion on how he can make this a more fun way of inspecting the houses.

(Q): With your role as CEO of the company and with your vast knowledge about technology and systems, what would you recommend in making inspections more fun and more effective?

(A): Thank you for asking for my opinion on this topic. I think that this is an area where we can be more innovative. Let's imagine this picture – You wake up in the morning, do your research, compile your list of addresses, and now you're ready to go. Instead of dressing up professionally you dress up in exercise clothes. You drive to the first address and park the car a block or two away. Get your smartphone ready with your headset and start walking toward the property. Turn on a voice recording application and record the information on the property as you walk and look. This way you get your daily exercise while recording the information without raising any concerns and have the information accurately recorded at the same time.

This approach has worked for me in many cases before when I was doing sales and needed to get cold marketing contacts. I use exercise as a common theme in talking with other people. There might be people that are exercising at the same time so I talk with them asking them about the walking or running route that they would recommend. I was able to turn a cold market into a warm market and I think this approach would work well for you and your inspection team.

One piece of the puzzle in bidding for the house is the way we determine which property we should be focusing on at the time of bidding and how much to bid. The inspection team has the opportunity to describe other conditions not at the heart of the property but the surrounding area and this is as important as the condition of the property.

When I first looked into the process, I did not know how to evaluate a good area from a bad area. I look at all locations to be the same and the reason is because I lacked the attention that was needed. This is referencing back to the demographic topic in chapter three above in learning the good, the bad, and the ugly about the area you are about to invest in. The inspection team shared with me their way of evaluating the surrounding location.

As you're driving through a location, pay attention to the way the cars are parked. Do you see many parked cars? How are they parked? What type of cars are they? If you see that **there are** many cars nicely parked, most of the cars are high-end cars, and the cars are well-maintained then the location is good because it indicates that the people living here have a good income bracket, they have a job, and the value of the properties here have good potential to rise. In addition you also need to pay attention to identify the safety of the area. If you know an area where the owner parked their car on the street instead of inside the garage this indicates that the location is safer and well taken care of by the people living there.

As the inspection team drives to the property, one of the responsibilities is to pay attention to the nearby school types (high school, elementary, etc.), the local market (Luckys, Safeway, Wal-Mart, etc.), and if there is a nearby cemetery or not. These criteria are important to different buyers' culture. For example, Asian buyers would not like to live nearby a cemetery because they believe the bad spirits will keep them from being prosperous or healthy. On the other hand, the western culture may not believe these types of superstitions.

If the properties you are about to acquire are in the location conditions above then they are great candidates to bid on or make an offer on. Please refer back to previous chapter so that you can ensure to get the property at the lowest price.

I am going to change my view point a little to show you the other side of the coin. Let's say you saw a property that is in a bad location such as the location had many broken cars parked on the streets for months, the street is not as clean, and the houses are not being maintained. Would you think about acquiring a property there? Most investors or novice investors would not even look at them just because of the location conditions. As an expert investor, you would always at least take a look because of the reasons below:

1.   Follow the rule "Don't judge a book by its cover."

2.   You can get the property for the lowest price because there is no one bidding on the house.

As long as you do your research and if the property shows good profits then it is the right property to acquire.

Chapter 5

Do Your Due Diligence

N THIS CHAPTER WE WILL BE COVERING THE RECORD KEEPING, THE tax lien researching, the loan document data, receipt tracking, escrow process, preparation for listing, and collecting the payments. Just looking at the tasks themselves one can imagine how critical this chapter would be for your business. With that said, please read this chapter carefully. Here is another bonus for you in regarding to record keeping. To obtain this bonus, go to our web site at www.reiinvest. com and share your input about the process described in this chapter and share with us what can be improved. We will send you a week free trial of our project planning system where you can manage the entire process from the time you acquired the property to the time you collect the payment from selling the property. Make sure you include your name, phone number, and email address for us to send you your free trial login credentials.

Our conversation is with Ana and Quyen who are the two Senior Data Analysts of our company. Their role is to maintain the auction database in the manner of keeping the data up-to-date in perspective of auctioning status, tax lien, back taxes, deed recording, maintaining the bought properties listing, and keeping the investors informed of the project status.

(Q): What does your typical day look like? What do you do first? What are the functionalities of your work? How does it impact the business?

(A): Wow – That's a lot of questions, Hung. Let me do my best in answering them for you.

- A typical day in general and high level would be entering the new property data into the REI system from data we extracted from third-party vendors provided to us, changing the status of the auction records that get postponed or cancelled for the day, and updating the description of the existing properties that are being auctioned for the day. There are two auction time frames for the county of Santa Clara, California. Ana handles the 10 AM listing and I am handling the 11 AM listing. We normally update these the night before so that the person who is doing the bidding will have the most up to date data to review.

- For our data entry, we do the auction record status update first, then move to entering the new data, gather the tax lien data and loan data to update existing properties, and research tax lien information for the new properties.

- The functionality is to keep everyone informed of the properties information, whether it is being auctioned in the current day or not.

- The accuracy of the data impacts the outcome greatly. I'd like to tell you a story where inaccurate data has cost us a lot of money. It was in 2011 and there was a property that was listed for auction in the zip code 95148, which is a new development area that's about 5 years old. In looking at the data the starting bid on the house was at $650,000 for four bedrooms, 2.5 baths, three-car garage, and with an in-law unit in the back. The price was outrageously low in comparison to the existing price on the market for that area. We researched and found that there is one property tax lien on the house, some back taxes, and one loan on the property. The tax lien amount was $51,000 and somehow it was entered in as $15,000 and we missed the second loan data of $75,000 and the data was not entered. The auction took place; we won the bidding at $725,000. The market for a similar property in the area was around $933,000. If everything was accurate we would have made a profit of $208,000 selling as is. But because of the data error, we ended up with the lower profit of $45,000 because we had to pay for all the liens and the second loan. That was a $163,000 loss just because our data was inaccurate.

(Q): You mentioned that you get data from third parties and you manually enter the data. What is that data and what data elements do they contain?

(A): One clarification please. We can do both manual data entry for short list and we leverage the mass data load (importing the data into the system) into REI system. The data elements are the typical data such are property owner name, address, contact info, the bank who currently owns the properties, the court house address, the auction date, the properties' short descriptions, properties' features such as number of beds, baths, year built, etc. But the most important data is the loan information such as if they sell the first loan position or they auction the second loan position. This data **must** be validated by multiple people and leveraged by multiple web sites.

In regards to websites, we use Foreclosure Radar (www.foreclosureradar.com), Auction.com (www.auction.com), and Priority Posting and Publishing Inc. (www.priorityposting.com). Auction.com is free but the other two are subscription-based. These websites provide us the data we need as the base.

(Q): You have so many places for the data and you indicate the risk of inaccurate data above. How would you ensure the data is accurate? Is the data you get from the sources above accurate? What do you do to reconcile the data?

(A): Firstly, with the database and with the websites, we check to see if the data exists on both listings of Foreclosure Data (FD) and

Priority Posting and Publishing (PPP) or not. We only add in the new data as needed and if the data is not in both of the lists from FD and PPP. We put in the new property because every week there is new property that comes out that has an auction date on the sale. After we complete this and both lists are the same then we do the auditing of the property that will be postponed to the future auction date. Then we will do research on whatever is left on the list.

There's also a difference between the sources we use. Let's say Blue Sheet (BS) gives us more information; they'll let us know whether the property has a pool. That's very important because that contributes to the cost of our construction of how much we have to deduct from our bid so that we can make up that cost right there. Or we can know right away whether the property is one-car garage or two-car garage. So that's the difference between BS and the other sources we would add to our database. BS gives us more information on the property details whereas FR gives the basic information and loan information.

The third party vendor can make mistakes, too, and we would get wrong data from the vendor such as incorrect property details and sometimes they give us incorrect addresses. In this case we refer back to Zillow (www.zillow.com) to correct and synchronize the data.

(Q): So far we talked about how to get the basic property details and loan information. What about the taxes and/or the lien related to the properties?

(A): Great segue way into this topic. The context here is pertaining to Santa Clara county of California. The information and regulations will be different from state to state and from county to county. As you know California is a strange state. Please make sure you refer to the rules and regulations of your own area.

The website is called Santa Clara County (www.santaclaracounty. org). Please keep in mind that most government websites get changed without notice to the public so make sure you verify the website before spending too much time researching.

Even though we can use the website to do the research, we prefer doing research real-time because the data at the court house is much more accurate than on the website. The court house system gets updated with the data first and then it will disburse to other supporting systems. The problem with spending the time at the court house is you need to be consistent with your timing of arriving and leaving to avoid upsetting the clerks. They are your best friends so stay on their good side. We get there normally after lunch around 1:30 pm. Take a number if there is a machine in your county court house and wait for your number to be called. You have a limited time frame to use the court house system so make use of the time wisely. Prepare questions that need to be asked of the clerks because some of the data is not yet entered into the system and is most likely be in the form of a hard copy. Make a list of the properties you are researching for the day and make sure you have the assessor's parcel number (APN) handy because the address can be entered incorrectly and the APN is the key to the court house database system.

We research on an average of 10 to 20 properties a day and by the time the auction dates come around, we can finish 3 to 7 properties on a good day.

Once we get the raw data into the system, we need to monitor the data and make sure the auction status is up to date to avoid wasting time on unnecessary data. Both Ana and Quyen review a listing of 80 to 100 properties daily and from there they would change the status of the auction properties to postponed or cancelled so that they can focus directly on the actual properties. Even these properties can be postponed or cancelled at the last minute.

Additionally, they review the properties' description to ensure the data is accurately entered by the field inspector, auctioneer, and themselves by reviewing the information, move the tax lien or any detail that may impact the opening bid and the max bid amount up to the top of the description so that the auctioneer has firsthand real-time visibility of the data at the court house bidding.

Let me share with you a story so that you can understand the lesson we are trying to teach.

It was early April of 2012 and the property tax was about to be due on the property located on Kelso Ct., San Jose, CA 95127. The house was on the bidding list beginning at $225,000. We had done our homework so we knew the property could be sold at around $405,000 and we knew about the $70,000 tax lien on the property. This information allowed us to bid up to a maximum of $295,000. A few other auction-goers were bidding against us and one of them ends up getting the property at $375,000. They didn't find out about the lien until later so they lost money instead of making money. The point of the story is you need to make sure you cover all bases and provide your bidder with the best information there is. This information allows the bidder to make informative decisions when bidding on the house. We will discuss bidding behavior in more depth in the following chapter.

In talking with Ana and Quyen I found out some tips and tricks in dealing with the county record office and thought it is valuable for you to know. Let's see what they had to say.

(Q): If someone asked to be your apprentice, what advice would you give them?

(A): Be very diligent with your data entry, of course, and also be very detailed; it doesn't need to be done as fast as people think. We're all human and everyone makes mistakes. So always check your work because one mistake from you could cost our company hundreds of thousands of dollars. Just be cautious, always double check your work, be diligent in what you do and always have motivation to do it; it's very time consuming and very tiring because you spend most of the time on the computer. You're logging in and out at random times of the day so just be patient.

Another rule of thumb is "don't assume." Don't assume that the lien does not belong to the house but rather double check or triple check so that you can avoid losing hundreds of thousands as mentioned above.

(Q): Are there any tips for working with the government system and personnel? For example with the county clerk's office, are there any tips in terms of working with the people there so that they can be nicer to you and be helpful to you?

(A): Of course there are tips and tricks. We always have them.

- Tip number 1: As I mentioned before in regards to timing, be at the record office at least 1 hour prior to closing, which is at 4:30 pm. When I say closing I mean closing because the system will automatically shut down.

- Tip number 2: Make friends with the clerks and other researchers because you're going to be seeing them 3-4 times a week and you will get to know these people regardless. When you're working in the research area, you're working with other competitors; you're working with other people that are out at the record office for the same properties as you are and looking for the same information that you are. They're not just there to look up their own properties; they're out there looking for other information that can be to their advantage. So of course, you can be friends with them, talk to them, ask them for pointers and they'll give you hints on how they do it and you can return a favor by sharing but keep your secret sauce tucked away. They said "you'd rather have your enemy close." You **must** (not should) be friendly with the people that manage the area, re-spect their space as well. Ask them about their weekend, their family, etc. This will benefit you in a big way.

- Tip number 3: Pay close attention to the number of names on the title. The common mistake is they only see the first person on the title when they look through the deed system. If you are not doing due diligence and checking all the names on the deed against the lien, you will easily miss something and put the property in jeopardy and this is a very, very dangerous place to be. This type of lien can be placed on any assets you have.

- Tip number 4: Don't take shortcuts but rather do everything the way it's done traditionally. Make sure you fill in all the blanks regarding data unless you know for certain that the data is not available. Once you have learned the traditional way, from then on you can find ways to enter the data much faster. For example: Before we just used the blue sheet and entered every piece of data. Now we utilize foreclosure radar and we cut and paste so the process is much faster. We can do this because we did it the traditional way and we know what's missing with the data. Only do shortcuts once you have mastered the process.

For someone who is new to the trustee and/or foreclosure process, knowing about the different types of tax liens will help you know how to manage them accordingly. These tax liens can be placed on your assets. You will learn which liens expire, which will not, and which can cause big problems for you.

(Q): In your research, how many types of tax liens are there and what should we be concerned with in dealing with tax liens?

(A): There are many types but it does not make sense to cover them all here. We will share with you the most common types and you can research more on your own. Additionally, it is different from state to state. We are not certified in this field and whatever we share is based on our working experience and knowledge. Please do not take this as the primary source of advice because it is not. We strongly recommend checking it with your local CPA or attorney for details.

- Property taxes are taxes based on your property values. They exist in all 50 states and the rate is different from place to place

- IRS taxes are taxes based on your annual income. There is federal income tax and state income tax.

- Mechanical taxes/liens are the unpaid services owed to the people or businesses that have done work on the property.

- Judgment lien is the type of lien caused by an order of the court due to the outcome of a law suit.

- Home Owner Association (HOA) is for unpaid HOA dues.

- Pending law suit is a lien that is pending court order upon a verdict.

- City Violation is a penalty from not following protocol and not having proper permits when altering your property.

- Utilities lien is for unpaid electricity and gas bills.

- Garbage lien is for unpaid garbage bills.

- Water lien is for unpaid water bills.

(Q): Is there a way that we can check on these liens and see if they can be removed or waived?

(A): Yes, there is a way and it requires that you read the actual documents, which you can find at the county record office system. The document format does not allow you to search for keywords to speed up the research. With that said, you have to read the document page by page. This is a tedious and time-consuming process. The document has a document number which we often use to verify and pair up the release document. You can find the release date or time period for waiving or dropping the lien.

Please note the above is applicable to liens that still belong to the government. If it has been sold to a private person, the private person who owns the lien must give the permission to release it first before you can drop the lien from the property.

There are liens, such as mechanical liens, that have an expiration date. The lien holder must request an extension for the lien to continue being active. If not, the lien will be automatically being dropped off after a certain number of days. Once again I caution you that this information is for California only. The fundamental is the same but double-checking with certified people is best. Your title company will know about the lien on the property because they need to issue title insurance or owner's title insurance and they cannot issue the insurance if there are liens on the property. With that said, the title company can help find out about the active liens or liens that have been released or dropped off.

(Q): You mentioned the document that contains all the liens information. Where can one find that document?

(A): At the county office, the clerk recorder's office in the public research area. There you would use the computer to open the documents where you will find all the information such as who filed the lien and the exact amount of the lien. You can check online for these documents; however, the document is a limited version and will not disclose full details. I am assuming a similar system is available at different counties in different state.

With all the work the team does, from the time the data gets entered into the system, to inspecting the house, updating the record, getting the comparable values, determining the profit gap, and checking on the liens, there is one process that **must** be completed by the man himself, which is Khoa. The process is called the final review and he does this ritually every night before the auction.

He goes through the auction properties one by one and reviews the data carefully. He starts with the property description, which he reads word-for-word, and zeroes in on the information written. Because he has done this for so many years it becomes second nature to him. He can easily spot any concerns if there are any. If there is he would then turn to Zillow (www.zillow.com) or Trulia (www.trulia.com) to find the information needed. The information he seeks is to determine the maximum bid on the property. With the information acquired, he puts it aside and moves into the liens section. He reviews the information gathered by the Senior Data Analyst. He uses a special tool, which only he has the information to connect to. This tool allows him to review deeper into the loan information and gather additional data for his decision about the property. There are situations where the second loan amount is not visible and with that tool he was able to find out more about the second loan. He spends a good two hours with this process. For each property he then begins the color code process. He marks with blue the properties with great potential. The properties that play the role of a backup buy are marked with yellow. The property should not be considered if he marks it with red because of the high risk and low profits.

These techniques are developed over the year through failures and successes. Khoa has leveraged these techniques to build an empire for himself and is able to support many people who are currently working for him.

If such a coaching program exists where Khoa teaches you the process step-by-step, wouldn't that interest you? If the answer is yes, here is your fourth bonus. Login to our website (www.reiinvest.com) and using "Contact Us," write us an email expressing your interest. We will provide one 30-minute meeting with Khoa to determine if the coaching is a fit for you. This is a complementary meeting with the owner, Khoa Le, and with the co-owner/CEO, Hung Q. Do.

Chapter 6

The court house courtesy

THE SUN HAS NOT YET RISEN BUT I'VE BEEN AWAKE AND HAVE spent some time reviewing the auction list for the very last time and I know that my partner is doing the same. In Santa Clara County we have trustee sales two to three times a day, five days a week (excluding holidays of course). My partner always is the first to arrive at the court house. He would sit in the car and visualize the court house from yesterday's event to see who the returned bidders are and who the new bidders are. I noticed that and one day I asked him what is the purpose of that exercise and he shared with me his thoughts.

The purpose for the exercise is two-fold: 1) is to meditate and to focus on the topic of auctioning and 2) is to better understand your competitors. The reason you need to pay attention to your competitor is because you need to anticipate their move, their bidding behavior, their code of conduct, and much more.

Most of the bidders are individual investors who are self-employed and are doing this to earn extra income. Their experience is limited and cumbersome because they do not have the resources and the tools like we do. Their tool is a hard copy of the Excel spreadsheet with the information they have gathered days ago which can be out dated. Knowing this we can anticipate their moves and most often they are very reserved which means they are bidding but bidding with uncertainties and fear.

The bidding habit is somewhat important to pay attention to. Are they constantly increasing the bidding or are they jumping all over the place? Do they respond to the increase fast or slow? Do they talk on the phone during the bidding? This behavior indicates that they could be doing the bidding for someone else who does not wish to be known.

Are they bidding on a particular zip code or does it matter? This provides an indication that they are not focused and might not have the details needed to make sound decisions.

Knowing these behaviors from the competitors, you can predict the outcome of the biddings. For zip codes you want to control, you will bid to get the property and to control the pricing. There are times you will need to increase your bid quickly so that your competitor cannot follow.

I would like to share with you a story that I had the opportunity to observe during one of the auctioning events. Please note in the beginning, the bidders did not know who I am or who I was working with. A few struck up conversations with me. I calmly told them that I am thinking about getting into the business and just observing the process so that I can decide to move forward or not. During the conversation, one of the gentlemen started to point out the bad behavior of the other bidders. I kept quiet and listened patiently. The auction began so everyone kept quiet to listen to the auctioneer. As the bidding was going, the auctioneer called the next bid three times. As the auctioneer announced the third calling, a new bid came in slightly after the third announcement. The person who thought he had the bid increase was surprised when the auctioneer informed him that he was too late. He started to speak in a loud voice and challenged the auctioneer's decision and he called the auctioneer names. Everyone there was amazed at the behavior he presented. He did not win the bidding but from that moment on people began to discontinue carrying a conversation with him as they had been before. People seemed to step away when he approached.

In trying to study people, I pretended that I was new and would like to know about other people. I asked around about Khoa, my partner. Most responded that he is friendly and he does not present himself as a know-it-all but rather shows that he does not know much. The other bidders know that he has a system and he has the knowledge; however, he always treated them with a smile and provided help when needed.

Not only does being respectful help you succeed at the trustee sales, but it will get you ahead of the game in any business. Downplaying yourself does not mean you are weaker than the others but rather opening yourself to more learning from within and from others.

I'd like to take this moment to explain the auctioning process for those that have never been to a trustee sales auctioning before. Please note that the rule changes slightly from county to county. For Santa Clara County, you need to have your driver's license and either a cashier's check or a bank check in order to participate in the bidding. You must register with the auctioneer prior to the bidding beginning. The bidding and winning bid are final transactions. You cannot cancel the winning bid once it has been finalized. The bank, however, can cancel the sale. In that case, your money will be refunded to you.

During the bidding process, you can increase in any amount you like and the bank can also bid with a small increase. In observing my partner at the auction, I noticed that he pays attention to the people who register for the property he is interested in. Since we have done our homework we know exactly how much we will bid on a property and therefore we can take control of the bidding. However, I notice that sometimes he lets the other person win the bidding because he feels that the other person can benefit more, especially if he has more than one property to bid on for that day. However there are zip codes that he would always want to win the bidding for, like a lion that has marked their territory and always wants to protect it. In this case he would hold out and get the property.

Once you have won the bidding and the purchase paperwork has been done, it would take two days for the record to complete. Here is our conversation with Ana who is responsible for the property until the closing.

(Q): Once we have purchased a trustee property, what are the steps that need to be taken?

(A): Once the property has been bought, the steps are:

1. Purchase home owners insurance. This is important because if we do not have home owner insurance, we will not be covered at all. Even though we try our best, things do happen. We had bought a trustee sales property in Las Vegas on a Friday afternoon. As soon as we had completed the paperwork, our Field Manager contacted the main office in California to purchase the home owner insurance but for some reason it was not completed in time by the insurance company; the property was burned over the weekend. With no insurance, we had to do a full rebuild of the property, out of our own pocket. The lesson learned here is to always have a local insurance company to work with so that home owner insurance can be purchased on the same day to protect your investment.

2. Wait for the trustee deeds to come to us so that we can do the recording.

3. After we are done with the recording, we turn it over to the property management for evictions if the property is occupied either by tenants or previous owners. The property management team performs the eviction process in parallel with the deed recording.

4. Once the property is vacant, we begin the construction estimation and the repair design. Then the construction starts.

5. Perform the final inspection and stage the property.

6. Listing the property.

The above steps are in summary and because we have a system that manages the whole project, we do not need to elaborate on the steps with the exception of the eviction process.

It is difficult for people to accept that they are losing their home and with feelings of anger and sadness, they're capable of reacting badly, even though you're trying to help them.

Last year, we had a case where a person came to us asking for help in saving his home from being foreclosed. We met with the family, learned about the family's hardships, and we worked out a plan to overcome the problem. The plan was put in place to be executed. The family then deviated from the plan and somehow could not get the refinance process and could not save the house. The house was on the trustee list and we thought that we would help them the second time so we purchased the property and then sold it back to the family. Once again they could not pass the loan so we had no choice but to ask them to leave. Instead of appreciating our efforts in helping, they returned the favor by trashing the property. They took a chain saw and cut the entire interior wall along with the electrical inside the wall. They dumped cement in the toilet and they assembled a broken car in the middle of the living room. They painted graffiti all over the house. It just goes to show that things happen and we can choose to handle it in a calm manner and we will be on top.

In looking at the process of eviction, I would like to share with you some of my thinking but please note that I am not an expert in property management and the eviction process. I just want to share some common sense on the subject of eviction.

We all know that the emotional stress is extremely high for those that are about to lose everything that is dear to their heart if they are the owner of the property. For tenants, the emotional stress is still there but at a lesser degree.

Toward the end of summer in 2012, we bought about 15 properties in Las Vegas. Out of those 15 properties, 3 of them were trashed greatly. I did some research by talking with the nearby neighbors in asking them about the people who previously lived in the home. I found out that those people were gentle and kind. They were in a bad situation and were evicted without any assistance which is why they were angry and trashed the property.

At this point I would like to share a few tips on how to deal with previous owners and/or tenants. The above stories tell us that desperate people do desperate things and most often they are negative things such as graffiti, broken windows, destroy toilets, etc. This is not a win-win position for both parties. The tenants are leaving in anger with no assistance and the new property owner is stuck with a huge construction fee.

At the next property where we needed to evict the tenants, here is what we had done and it created a win – win position. The couple was in their early 30's with two children at the age of 2 and 4. The wife is a home maker and the husband was working for a manufacturing company. The reason we know this is because as soon as we bought the property, we did our homework to find out as much as we could about the tenant by talking to the neighbors and by talking to the tenant. Our actions showed that we care and we are trying to offer a helping hand. We asked our property management team to treat them with respect and understanding. We came there with a few job leads (we leverage our connections in this matter), and we offer cash for keys. The amount is enough for the tenants to find a new place or have a place to stay for the children. They much appreciated the gesture and were happy to accept the offer. The husband found a new job not from our lead but triggered by it. We tried this approach going forward and found it works 80% of the time and has saved us tons of construction money.

You are probably wondering how we handle the other 20%. With the giving and understanding mindset, we ask our attorney to work with the tenant in the same manner but firmly. The attorney completes an eviction letter which includes a clause that we are willing to negotiate for the benefit of both parties. This leads to another 10% contacting us before we have to serve the eviction letter and involve police officers.

Chapter 7

Shock and Awe

IN THIS CHAPTER, I AM SHARING WITH YOU THE PROJECT MANAGEMENT system from the time you receive the key to the property to the time you complete staging the property and are ready to display your hard work to the public and make a quick and profitable sale.

Kim Nguyen and Sophia Nguyen are our construction and design team who are responsible for the rehab of the properties from beginning to end. They have tips and tricks that can help guide you through the process with ease.

(Q): In your experience, what are some of the best techniques in selecting a construction crew(s)?

(A): Thank you for starting your interview with this question because I personally feel that this is the most important question that must be answered before you even start venturing into the rehab property business. The three answers to this question are:

1. Time – You will be saving a lot of time from the design time, planning time, dealing with city planning department time, and actual construction time.

2. Money – Having a great and reliable construction crew saving you money because they know where to get the best supplies,

used or new equipment, and they do not misrepresent the labor cost.

3. Satisfaction – You, as the customer of the construction crew, will be happy because the crew understands what you want, delivers what you need, and completes to your time line.

Let me clarify the term "construction crew." It means that you must have an architect, a licensed general construction company, and multiple specialized handymen working for you. This does not mean you have only construction companies working for you but rather multiple specialized teams so that smaller projects can be handled by handymen and leaving big projects for a construction company. You can save a lot of money working this approach. In addition, construction companies can also be focused on development projects versus small projects where the cost from a construction company can be double or sometimes triple the cost of a handyman.

Finding a good construction crew and/or handymen is like hiring an employee for your company. The best source is when friends or trusted relations refer the construction crew to you. The next best source is from previous working relationships. Regardless of which approach you take there are four key things you look for in a construction company:

1. Trustworthy – Does the construction company do what they say? Do they deliver on their promises?

2. Accountability – Do they take pride in their work? Do they double check their work? Are they perfectionists or do they work only for the money?

3. Follow instruction – How are they in following instructions?

4. Professionalism – Do they provide you best market practices for the construction field? Do they provide options and explain the options for you clearly?

With the four items above, it is best to always interview the construction crew and/or handymen. Give them the opportunity to demonstrate their abilities to you by asking them questions, giving them a task to do, and asking them to deliver things to you in a few days. Here are some sample questions:

1. Please tell me about a recent project you worked on. What did the project entail and what were the details of your deliverable tasks? What percentage of those tasks did you deliver? Give me specific examples of the quality you provide.

   a. The expected behaviors are presented to you about the project with specific details which demonstrate they are paying attention to details, communicate precisely, and honestly answer your question.

2. Do you mind providing a list of references? Could you send the list to me in about three days from now (call out a specific date)?

   a. The expected behavior is following your instruction and keeping the promise.

3. Let's say I came to you and asked you to reconstruct my kitchen which was tile, electric stove, pine wood cabinet, and has room for an island with sink in the middle. What would be your advice to me?

   a. The expected answer here is to show you that they know the regulations of the city, telling you what needs permit or doesn't need permit, and provide options along with advantages and disadvantages of having the island in the middle of the room.

   b. It also shows how serious they are in wanting to work with you. If they take the time to provide the information then they are serious with their work, otherwise they will brush off the answer and will not give you the information you need.

4. Let's come back to the example you mentioned in question 1. You show the work to your client and while you are showing you notice some defects such as the light fixture is not properly installed, the paint is not clean or is missing in some areas, or the moldings were not cleanly joined. What would you do in this case?

    a. The expectation here is for them to honestly call out the flaws, making the note, provide a date when it will be fixed, and most of all there should not be any cost involved. This shows that they take pride in their work and accept accountability for their job.

You can use the above questions as a basis to come up with more questions that might be unique to your situation. During the interview, I do not recommend talking about cost or fees. You should ask if they have a store saving program that can help lower the cost for clients.

(Q): These are great tips. Can you give us the high level process and then go into details for each step of the rehab process?

(A): Some of the steps I am about to share might be a repeat from above; however, it is important to repeat. In summary, the steps are:

1. Buy home owner insurance – Senior Data Analyst

2. Record the deed – Senior Data Analyst

3. Get the keys (Eviction is a separate task and done by the eviction team) – Senior Data Analyst

4. Setup lockbox – Construction Coordinator

5. Taking the "before" pictures – Field Service Team

6. Estimate the construction – Construction Coordinator

7. Select the construction team or handyman for the job – Construction Coordinator

8. Follow up picture taking – Field Service Team

9. Monitor the construction progress – Construction Coordinator

10. Final inspection – Construction Coordinator

11. Staging the property – Construction Coordinator

12. Taking the "after" pictures – Field Service Team

13. Communicate with Realty Company to list the property – Senior Data Analyst. Next chapter will go into detail on this point.

I will skip step 1, 2, and 13 because they are either repeated from previous chapters or will be covered by the next chapter.

Setup the lockbox – A few people came up to me and asked "Why do we need to do this? Should the key be kept by one person to avoid breaking in?" The answer is that there are times we need other people to complete their job before we can do our job. Having the lockbox prevents bottleneck and delay of the process and gives other people free access to the property. Regarding the security of the property, the lockbox has a code and only the people who know the code can gain access to the property. The code should not be given out freely. The construction coordinator should be the person who provides the code and **must** select who to give the code out to. The best practice is to change the code every 30 days or 60 days. Another best practice is to have a code setting system. Using a portable alarm system is also a good practice for the property with the least construction or with a high value because you do not wish to have more damage to the property. Sometimes by having just the security sign in front of the house can reduce the chance of vandalism by 10% to 20%.

Taking the "before" pictures – The best marketing tool is to show the potential customers what they are getting, what big values they are receiving from the house, and pictures say a thousand words. These pictures capture the house as it was before we do any reconstruction to the house. The pictures also provide evidence of fixing to investors, if being asked for. I am going to cover picture-taking techniques in this section as well so that you can capture the right pictures for your collection.

Taking pictures is an art form and some education is needed in order to take great and meaningful pictures. We are not asking you to be a professional photographer but we do ask that you let your creativity run free so that you can see the hidden beauties in your vision. Most of the time we focus too much on our daily activities such as finding deals, showing new homes, finding the potential issue with a newly bought home, figuring out the construction cost, etc. and we push our creativities into the backseat. The process should be reversed because the creative part of our brain is the part that releases the daily stress, brings a smile to our faces, lets the inner child come out to play, and, most of all, keeps our dreams alive. So let your imaginations run wild at least one to two days a week.

What would you need for the picture-taking process? You and a decent camera are all you need for this task. I do not recommend taking pictures with your smartphone's camera because they do not give you the best images. A decent camera costs around $100 to $150 nowadays so invest in one to capture clear pictures to tell your story about the home.

There are two fundamental points to my picture-taking approach: 1) From the outside in and 2) general pictures to detailed pictures. Let me expand on these two points for clarification.

Do you sometimes stand in front of the mirror and look at your hair, your face, your clothing? I would bet every one of us have done this at least once in our life time. What do we see when we do this? There are times we also stand in front of the mirror and look at our stomach, our muscles, and our chest. We then say the stomach is too big, the muscle is too flimsy, and it gives us ideas on how to fix things. Looking at our hair, our clothing this is the process of "**outside in.**" We start with the outside looking at the street view and let the picture tell the investor how safe or busy it is at a certain time of the day. We look at the front of the house, the side of the house, the lawn, the garage, the windows, the porch, the back yard, and more. We want to complete the outside first before we move inside of the house. When we're ready to move inside, we always want to start from the front door and let the view start from left to right in a clockwise motion. You then capture the view of the front door hallway, the living room, the family room, the kitchen, the bath room, the bed room, the closet, and so on.

Similar to above, there are times you would look at yourself from afar to see the overall view of your face then you notice a spot under the eye and wonder what that is so you move in closer to take a better look. This is called "**general to detail**." You want to take a picture that captures the big and whole view of the house first because it is the beginning of your story. The general view is like the "Once upon a time in the small city called …." of your story. I strongly recommend taking about two to three pictures of the front of the property in different angles to give your viewers the 3D effect view point. Once the general has been taken then you now need to focus on the details such as how the front door looks up close, if a new coat of paint would brighten up the porch, etc. You repeat this process for everything outside first then go inside. The same concept applies to taking the pictures inside.

Here are a few tips that you might want to pay attention to because they are often the most expensive part of the construction.

- Take the picture of the ceiling and floor to look for signs of damage.

- Take the picture of the plumbing underneath all the sinks and look for signs of leakage.

- Take the picture of the cabinets with all the doors opened to see the cleanliness of the inside, and look for signs of molding and/or moistures

- Take the picture of the bath room and the plumbing.

As I mentioned above, you always let your view go clockwise, take a wide angle view picture, and then zoom into the area that needs special attention such as punctures in the wall, scratches on the hard wood floor, ripped carpet, damaged outlet, etc.

My recommendation for this simple activity is having one person doing a property so that the process can be repeated by the same person when taking the "after" pictures.

Estimate the construction effort – Most of the tasks in this part of the rehab process require a lot of imagination because it allows you to make the property a very special home for someone. At this point, there are two roles in your organization that are needed here. They are the inspector and construction coordinator. The inspector is responsible for inspecting the condition of the house and reporting back with fixing recommendations. The construction coordinator is responsible for the decisions as to what will be fixed, the designs for fixing, and how much budget will be involved in fixing.

The initial inspection of the property by the inspector will determine how much repair is needed. There would be a sheet of all inspection details itemized with the three statuses: 1) Poor, 2) Fair, and 3) Good. The sheet would also include a column for fixing with checkboxes for "Yes" or "No" and a comments section where the inspector would put his recommendation about the item. These statuses and comments allow the construction coordinator to decide which is needed to be fixed. To keep the process uniform, the inspection should follow the two approaches above: "outside in" and "general to details" to record the findings.

It would be best that your inspector has some knowledge of the requirements for FHA and conforming loans. If your inspector does not know about these requirements, I strongly recommend you send the inspector to training to gain this knowledge so that construction can be done properly and to avoid any delay in the loan process and selling process. Why do I mention the loan requirements? Let me share with you a story.

Four months ago we remodeled a house in the 94511 area (a San Jose, California zip code) where we needed to fix the kitchen, two bathrooms, the heating/air conditioning, and some minor electrical issues. The construction went well and it was done within the timeline and budget. We expected to have it sold in a few days. The offers were flying in like crazy and there were pre-approved loans of all types. One of the offers we accepted had an FHA loan and there were about 5 items on the list that the bank requested before it could be finalized. The five items are categorized in two major areas:

1) Safety

2) Functionality.

It sounds simple, doesn't it? Well it was not because the inspector did not pay attention to the items from the very beginning. During the loan approval inspection time, the bank inspector found the following problems:

1) There was grease in the filter of the stove hood

2) A quarter-inch gap in the front door

3) heating/air conditioning was not working properly

4) Two of the crawlspace screens were ripped

5) The pressure of the toilet was not up to standard pressure.

Items 1 and 2 are related to safety and items 3, 4, and 5 are a functioning issue. These items were quickly resolved but it delayed our final inspection from the bank by two weeks which went beyond the loan time limit for the buyer and the whole loan process got re-started. In the end, we sold the house not in a few days but in over two months. Would you be able to get a new property with the funds from this house if it was sold in time? The answer is definitely and we would have made more profit as well. The point I am trying to make is to take preventive measures, look at these potential road blocks up front, and avoid all of the delays I mentioned above.

Let's talk about how we should approach the construction cost estimation. The concept here is to get the most for your money and it is based on the desired outcome you would like to have with the property you have purchased such as: 1) Is the property in a high value neighborhood?, 2) Do we have any buyers that want to take over as is?, 3) Do you to want to keep the property or not?, and 4) How much profit would you like to get? Please keep in mind the value you put in will increase the selling value by 50% - 70% of the construction cost.

In the beginning of this chapter we talked about selecting your construction crew. One of the requirements you should ask for once you have selected the company is the unit price list where you can enter the data into your system. This will help expedite your estimation process. Please note that you might have different prices from different crews and/or from the handymen you have selected. My recommendation to you is to take an average price for your estimate. For example: For painting a room that's 100 – 150 square feet, Handyman A's price is $300. Handyman B's price is $400. Handyman C's price is $275. The average of $325 is your default estimate value that you enter into your estimation system if you have one. If you do not have one and would like to see a demo, connect to our website www.reiinvest.com and leave us an email and we will schedule a demo meeting with you.

Select the construction team for the job - The next three tasks 7, 8, and 9 are needed and they have been covered in previous chapters so I am going to summarize them here for ease of reading and following the process.

There are times when money should not be the road block for fixing the property because, as I mentioned before, you base your construction on different criteria. If you have a property that is in a high income neighborhood, spending a little extra will increase your property value tremendously. On the other hand, if you are fixing the property for renting, you might consider keeping the cost as low as you can and still maintain the quality of the fixing up. The important point I want to make here is always have a written detailed task list agreement from the construction company so that you know exactly what is being fixed and what is not and what the agreed unit price for each item is. This list will help you in so many ways from accounting, to final inspection, to maintaining great relationships with all the vendors.

During the construction, it is critical that you have the Field Service person swing by the property to see if there are any new developments worth recording. The normal schedule is about every two days. The responsibility of the Field Service person is to capture any new evidence of damages; it **is not** to provide instructions to the construction team. If it happens that the construction team asks, you should politely inform the person that you do not have any authority to make decisions regarding construction and leave it at that. The three areas that you will need to focus on most during this time are:

1. The kitchen

2. Bathroom

3. Bedroom

We want to see if there are any new damages that were not revealed from the initial inspection. If there are, we need to renegotiate with the construction team and/or with the investors.

At this time the construction coordinator is depending on the field service report for timely handling of the negotiation process and to stay in contact with the construction team regarding some of the defects the field service person is reporting. It is not a good idea to leave everything to the field service person; the construction coordinator should perform an unscheduled inspection as well. These are opportunities to see the construction team in action where you can evaluate their work, their work ethic, etc.

Khoa as the CFO and I as CEO periodically stop by to bring the construction team coffee and get to know the team. This is a great way to build relationship and trusts. The feedback we received is "It was very nice of them to come by, bring us drinks, and talk to us as their own employees." As you can see "happy employees make a happy and productive company."

Final Inspection – The construction coordinator often has done an inspection when the construction team has indicated that they have completed the job. The quality of the construction job has great impacts on your creditability with the buyers because if there are defects after we have sold the house, it will hurt our company image and brand. In addition, if we do not do a thorough inspection we will delay our selling process due to the requirements from the bank.

We use the same document for the final inspection as we do at the initial inspection and fixing indication because they are related. I strongly recommend keeping them in one document to make the tracking process simple and easy to manage. The document is shared and can be accessed by everyone. With the items agreed upon to be fixed, the inspector can pay more attention to those items. The objective is to inspect everything regardless if there was work done or not. Sometimes the littlest things are the biggest headache for you. Here are some of the most common errors in the inspection:

1. The door lock for each and every door of the house should be working and you should be able to close and lock the door. In one of the properties we found the bathroom door could not be closed because the lock was installed incorrectly. How would the buyer feel once they have moved into the house and discovered this kind of defect?

2. The electricity, lights, outlets, and fan should be working.

3. The water is on and there are no leaks in the kitchen sink, the bathroom sink, and the bathroom shower. Make sure you look underneath the sinks.

4. The water flow in the toilet should be strong and there should be no sign of blockage.

5. The garbage disposal should work properly.

6. The furnace and water heater should be securely fastened, working, and the pilot light must be on.

7. The heating/air conditioning should work properly.

8. There should not be any grease in the kitchen range hood.

If there is it should be cleaned or replaced because it is a fire hazard and will be rejected by FHA loan.

9. Make sure the property is clean and clear of garbage.

10. Make sure the sprinkler systems are working.

11. Ensure the garage door is working properly and have proper safety control installed.

This is a subset of our inspection system. If you take pride in your work, it will reflect in the satisfaction of your customers and happy customers mean a growing business. The definition of "branding" is the customers' view of your company. Final inspection is an opportunity to introduce the "wow" factor to your customers.

Staging, the "after" picture, and let the selling begin – I am about to share a few general thoughts about decorations and the effectiveness of using space, objects, and light to stage your property to get the best attraction during the day or at night.

You can decorate the house with no specific style at all, as long as you are satisfied with it. However, if you want to give your living space a stylish, truly luxurious, and, above all, a comfortable feel, you should decorate in a certain style. Therefore, before you decide to decorate a room or a house, you need to determine whether you want it to reflect any furniture, accessories, colors, and layouts suitable for your selected style.

Themed Decorations – Every little corner in your house can be a different decorative theme by incorporating decorative accessories into a group. The decoration of each thematic group will help you limit the decorative items and focus attention on the space where you want to emphasize. However, you should note that each room should have only a few highlights in the space that you love or desire to be seen.

Cool and Pleasant Space – Trees and their bright green color help the house look more serene and pleasant. It also helps the living space to be closer to nature. To decorate the room this way, you can use flowers that include many green leaves such as lilies or roses, with a lot of ferns. If you do not have the opportunity for flowers or plants, you can use vases of many styles and shapes in the same color tone to brighten the room. Please note that there are colors that bring coolness such as blue, green, grey, etc. There are colors that bring warmth such as red, orange, yellow, etc. If necessary, you can add fresh flowers in the vases for a livelier environment.

Knowing your space and furniture – The furniture layout can be small or large, depending very much on the space. The smaller the space, the less room to display your furniture and if you decorate with large furniture items, it will definitely make the space feel crowded. As for open space, using colored blocks and large items makes the room quiet and more comfortable.

See into space – Use material you can see through or something that will appear further away. There are times you might not like having a large mirror in the room but before you remove it, please consider that the mirror may give the illusion of a large room. This is a good way to give yourself and guests the feeling of space, even if the room is small.

Colors and textures – The key to success in decorating is understanding and respecting the beauty of colors in combination with each other. When combining two colors such as black and white or red and gold, we need to pay attention to the harmonious proportions and the balance of the colors when deciding to paint the room. Here are the questions you need answers to. Which color should occupy more space in the room? How high or low should the colors rise from the floor? When we talk about the objects in a room, the same concept applies. Pay attention to the number of objects versus the height of painted color so that you can balance the color of the object and the color of the wall. You should always ask yourself one question, "Are the colors really appropriate for the room and for each other?"

Using pictures – Put the pictures' location at eye level. This will be more convenient for guests to admire your art works and create harmony with the surrounding furniture.

Create balance without symmetry – Another misconception is the picture, the image must be in the center of the hanging wall to ensure symmetry. But the reality is not so. The variations in asymmetry can sometimes create unexpected effects. For example, around the wall above the fireplace, paintings hung skewed to one side create an ideal location for a tall vase. This gives the balance of the picture and flowers.

Create a variety of heights – Choosing ornaments with different heights allows the observer to look at the decorations closer, slower, and spend time admiring the objects, rather than just glancing over them quickly. It also creates a sense of space and depth with more charisma.

Using lights – Light is one of the key elements in maximizing the effectiveness of the ornaments. Spotlights should be used to focus the attention to paintings, photographs, works of art, etc.

Something important that we often miss when we undo the staging is that we do not pay attention to the holes, the pieces of tape, or the small damages that may occur during our removal of the decorations. We strongly recommend that you pay attention to this so that it does not leave the buyer with an unsatisfied feeling when they move in and compare it back to the time of the open house. Again, happy customers are indications for a growing business.

Once the property has been staged, the construction coordinator informs the field service to take the after pictures of the house. The same concept discussed in the before picture should be used here because if you can replicate similar picture sets of the after as the before picture, the images will give the viewing audience a great deal of emotional feeling.

How do we use these pictures? One may ask. The answer is to create a marketing tool for investors and potential property buyers. Our marketing tool is the property portfolio where each portfolio is a property with the front as the cover, with the company logo, the property address, a few pictures of the property, and a catchy phrase about the property. The inside pages are used for showing the before (on the left) and the after (on the right) pictures. It is important to have the right pictures (which is why knowing how to take the pictures is important), design, and layout so it will be eye-catching to the investor or to the potential buyer. The back page is the property detail information such as number of square footage, number of beds, baths, schooling, shopping, parks, etc.

To the investors, you can provide the profit and exit strategies on how you acquired, remodeled, and sold the property in the past. This shows your professionalism, your dedication, and your work ethic with your investors.

To the potential buyers, you demonstrated to them the safety, the convenience, and the growth of the area. This shows that you care for and provide only the best quality to the life of your buyers.

Chapter 8

Sell Fast and Easy

NOW THAT YOU HAVE THE PROPERTY COMPLETELY DONE, IT IS ready for primetime showing. The question now is, should you sell or keep the property. What are the key factors that a business owner would look at in making this type of a decision? There are many but I would like to focus your attention to the following few when making your decision. You need to spend some time thinking about the following:

- Your business long term goals

- Your current assets

- Your revenue growth vision

Here are some of the leading questions that might help you in your strategic thinking process:

- What will my business look like 10 to 15 years from now?

- How many assets does the business have?
  - o If it is not much, what and how do we build the assets?
  - o If it is too much, what should we do to balance between assets and revenue?

- What does our quarter-by-quarter growth look like?

- What does our year over year growth look like?
- Would the bank loan us any money if we ask?

The answers to the above questions will guide you through your decision of selling or holding. Please keep in mind that a business will demonstrate growth and strength in the assets and not in the annual revenue. If you already have the assets established, I congratulate you. If it has not yet been established, it is recommended to hold the properties as your assets and use them to generate passive income for you.

Now let's switch the topic over to selling the property. As the construction coordinator finalizes the paperwork, a note is needed to inform the Senior Data Analyst and the accountant so that they can begin their processes.

The accountant needs to collect all expense receipts from the construction team, from the escrow team, from the investment team, and from the auction team. These receipts need to be tracked and prepared for collecting or paying, depending on the type of services. The accountant will cut checks to pay for construction services, paying interest to the investors, and deposit any payments received from other departments. The more accurate your book, the better position you are in.

The Senior Data Analyst will also begin their listing process. The best practice is to partner with a trusted realty company or better yet have a realty company of your own. Having a dedicated realty company gives you the benefits of having all the agents working for you at the same time versus having only one working at the time. In addition, you leverage their brand name to close the selling process as quickly as possible. The Senior Data Analyst will follow up on the listing, the offers received, provide counter offer details (please note that the Senior Data Analyst does not actually do the counter offer but rather leave it to the real estate agent) to the agents to counter back. The Senior Data Analyst will open an escrow account for each property, provide loan officers recommendations to agents to provide additional services to the buyers if needed, and answer questions for the investors in the prospect of closing on the property.

Our model is to share the profit with others and with that said, we do not claim any commission on the property; the selling agent will get all commission. This is one of the biggest contributions to our quick-selling benchmark.

Once the property has been closed, all paperwork, from the construction contract to the HUD, and everything related to the property must be collected, scanned, and stored in an external hard drive where it is kept outside of the office. This ensures that we protect the investors, the buyers, the sellers, and the company from misuse of data.

Chapter 9

Let's Celebrate

URING MY 20 YEARS OF WORKING IN THE CORPORATE WORLD, in consulting, or in the entrepreneur world, I have noticed that people do not take time to enjoy the success that they've achieved and that is a mistake that we all should rethink about our business.

"Successes lead to other successes" is a saying that I have heard from many business coaching sessions. In living the concept I can vow that it is true and is working tremendously well. May I share with you two stories about this? One is a personal story and one is a business-related story.

It was a spring day when we headed into Vietnam Town in San Jose, California for the New Year festival. I noticed the team had already arrived and was working on decorating the booth with our marketing materials, setting up the spinning wheel for prizes, and dividing the flyers to be handed out to the festival attendees. I noticed that all the banners had been carefully hung in the best places for people to see our logo and slogan, "Let your money grow with us." As the day went by, the line to our booth got longer and longer, the team was frantically handing out prizes that people won, signing people up for raffle tickets, and making balloon animals for the children. The music was playing with a lot of energy which brought more attention to our booth. All of the hard work has paid off by the length of the line to our booth. Other business participants were jealous of our success. Vietnamese celebrities came by our booth to take pictures with us. The media came by to interview us to find out more details about the company and about our successes. I noticed Johnny, my partner's son who is 7, he was there handing out prizes to the attendees. The festival ended with great success. We collected a list of over 600 names and numbers; these will be our prospective investors. Our company brand is now up a level with the Vietnamese community in the California Bay Area. Both Khoa and I were very big in celebrating our success so we organized a dinner get-together for everyone in our company to attend. During the dinner, we recognized all the people who participated and contributed to the company's success. Everyone enjoyed the dinner and the socializing. Two days after the dinner, I received many emails thanking us for giving the team the opportunity to enjoy. The team greatly appreciated the recognition from the executives for their hard work and they are looking forward to contributing more in the future events.

This is a personal story. It was early August 2013. I have landed in Vancouver, British Columbia at the airport and was picked up by a bus that would take us into the camp ground for Peak Potentials Enlightened Warrior Camp. That night we were introduced to the camp and the camp leader shared with us the smoking ground rule. I am a smoker so I paid special attention to the information. He then asked if we were willing to come on stage so I did. There he asked if we would be willing to stop smoking during the 5 days of camp. I agreed and so I took out the pack of cigarettes, broke them apart and tossed it in the trash can nearby. The whole camp of 375 plus people stood up cheering for us. It was a great feeling. I was doing very well the first night, the second night, and then the third morning the craving hit me but I fought back and was able to resist the temptation. I told my friend in my tribe and everybody stood up and gave me a standing ovation. The feeling was so great it kept me from smoking for the whole camp trip. On the third day another event happened to me. We were doing an exercise and I was exhausted and I could not move anymore. My partner took my backpack and carried it for me so that I could continue on. She dropped my backpack as we moved forward and three extra packs of cigarettes fell out of my backpack. She was surprised to find out that I still had cigarettes which I packed but did not touch. We both looked at each other and at that moment I made up my mind that I would quit smoking for good. We agreed to destroy the three packs of cigarettes together when we got back to camp. I did it in front of the tribe. During dinner I stood up and told everyone in the camp of my decision and I got another standing ovation but this time the whole camp stood up. It has been two months since I quit smoking and my tribe celebrates my success every 30 days with me. These little celebrations make me believe that I am strong, I can overcome any obstacles, and I can do anything. I celebrate every day that I do not smoke.

As you can see the power of celebrating your success and recognizing the team effort where it is due will lead you to more success and to a more powerful team because the team knows that you have their back, you treat them right, and you will always deliver on what you say. We do not need to wait for a big success to celebrate. We need to celebrate even on the small ones because it will generate the energy needed to achieve bigger success. I wish you all the best and I am ready to celebrate your success right now because you have bought this book and have read the book to the very end. I am dancing and cheering for you as you're finishing this book and beginning your very own new journey to richness.

Recognitions and Thanks

THIS BOOK HAS BEEN COMPLETED OVER MANY LONG DAYS AND LONG nights. I would not have been able to get here without the help of family, friends, and teammates. I would like to thank you all:

- Khoa Le – my partner for spending the time co-writing this book with me, in the area of trustee auctioning.
- Kim Phuong, Andrea Do, Andrew Do, and Austin Do – my wife and children for your encouragement with gentle reminders, hugs, and understanding for not being able to spend time with you during my book-writing.
- Marilyn Angelena – My business coach for sharing with me great tips about real estate and closing fund raising deals.
- Ana Lioi – My CEO coach for motivating me, changing my mindset, helping with controlling the little voice in my head by creating a contract with myself to get the book written.
- Anna Pham, Quyen Nguyen, Sophie Nguyen, Kim Nguyen, and Bang Nguyen – The REI team for sharing your knowledge and experiences which contributed awesomely to this book.
- Tony Do for all the graphic design work on the original book cover
- Raymond Aaron and his team – For showing me an opportunity to bring benefits to a lot of people with a book. Your guidance has allowed me to overcome my fear of writing. Your team has provided the services that I needed to be successful.

For this, I'm forever grateful for your relationships and helping hands.

Hung Q. Do & Khoa Le